50 Easy No-Bake Treats Recipes for Home

By: Kelly Johnson

Table of Contents

- Chocolate Peanut Butter Energy Balls
- No-Bake Cheesecake Bars
- Almond Joy Protein Bites
- Coconut Macaroons
- Rice Crispy Treats
- No-Bake Chocolate Oatmeal Cookies
- Strawberry Banana Nice Cream
- Peanut Butter and Jelly Bites
- Chia Seed Pudding
- No-Bake Oreo Truffles
- Energy-Boosting Granola Bars
- Chocolate-Dipped Fruit
- Vanilla Yogurt Parfaits
- Nutty Trail Mix Clusters
- Chocolate Avocado Mousse
- No-Bake Peanut Butter Pie
- Coconut-Lime Energy Bites
- S'mores Bites
- Date and Nut Balls
- Pumpkin Spice Bites
- No-Bake Lemon Bars
- Chocolate Coconut Bliss Balls
- Frozen Yogurt Bark
- Layered Pudding Cups
- Matcha Green Tea Energy Bites
- No-Bake Fruit Tart
- Chocolate Hazelnut Spread Dip
- Peanut Butter Chocolate Chip Dip
- No-Bake Rice Pudding
- Berry Coconut Smoothie Pops
- Chocolate-Covered Pretzel Bites
- Oatmeal Cookie Dough Bites
- Nut-Free Granola Bars
- No-Bake Banana Cream Pie
- Mint Chocolate Chip Energy Bites

- Chocolate Chip Cookie Pie
- No-Bake Chocolate Mousse Cups
- Peanut Butter Banana Sushi
- Cinnamon Roll Energy Bites
- No-Bake Tiramisu Cups
- Raspberry Coconut Bites
- Healthy Chocolate Fudge
- Caramel Apple Dip
- No-Bake Cherry Almond Bars
- Sliced Fruit with Nut Butter
- No-Bake Chocolate Chip Cheesecake
- Blueberry Coconut Chia Pudding
- Gingerbread Energy Bites
- Vegan Coconut Lime Truffles
- Chocolate-Covered Banana Bites

Chocolate Peanut Butter Energy Balls

Ingredients

- 1 cup rolled oats
- 1/2 cup peanut butter
- 1/4 cup honey or maple syrup
- 1/4 cup chocolate chips
- 1/4 cup ground flaxseed (optional)
- 1 teaspoon vanilla extract

Instructions

1. **Mix Ingredients:**
   - In a bowl, combine all ingredients and mix until well combined.
2. **Form Balls:**
   - Scoop out small portions and roll into balls.
3. **Chill:**
   - Refrigerate for at least 30 minutes to firm up.
4. **Store:**
   - Keep in an airtight container in the refrigerator for up to a week. Enjoy!

No-Bake Cheesecake Bars

Ingredients

- 1 cup graham cracker crumbs
- 1/2 cup melted coconut oil
- 2 cups cream cheese (or vegan alternative)
- 1/2 cup powdered sugar
- 1 teaspoon vanilla extract
- Fresh fruit or fruit sauce for topping

Instructions

1. **Prepare Crust:**
    - In a bowl, mix graham cracker crumbs and melted coconut oil. Press into the bottom of a lined baking dish.
2. **Make Filling:**
    - In another bowl, beat cream cheese, powdered sugar, and vanilla until smooth. Spread over the crust.
3. **Chill:**
    - Refrigerate for at least 4 hours or until firm.
4. **Slice and Serve:**
    - Cut into bars and top with fresh fruit or sauce before serving.

Almond Joy Protein Bites

Ingredients

- 1 cup dates, pitted
- 1/2 cup almonds
- 1/4 cup cocoa powder
- 1/4 cup shredded coconut
- 1 tablespoon almond butter
- 1 teaspoon vanilla extract

Instructions

1. **Blend Ingredients:**
   - In a food processor, combine all ingredients and blend until a sticky mixture forms.
2. **Form Bites:**
   - Scoop out portions and roll into balls.
3. **Chill:**
   - Refrigerate for at least 30 minutes to firm up.
4. **Store:**
   - Keep in an airtight container in the fridge for up to a week.

Coconut Macaroons

Ingredients

- 3 cups shredded coconut
- 1/2 cup sweetened condensed milk (or coconut cream)
- 1 teaspoon vanilla extract
- Pinch of salt
- 1/2 cup dark chocolate (optional, for dipping)

Instructions

1. **Preheat Oven:**
   - Preheat your oven to 350°F (175°C). Line a baking sheet with parchment paper.
2. **Mix Ingredients:**
   - In a bowl, combine shredded coconut, condensed milk, vanilla, and salt.
3. **Form Macaroons:**
   - Scoop out small mounds and place on the baking sheet.
4. **Bake:**
   - Bake for 10-12 minutes until golden brown.
5. **Cool and Dip:**
   - Let cool, then dip in melted chocolate if desired.

Rice Crispy Treats

Ingredients

- 6 cups rice cereal
- 1/2 cup butter or coconut oil
- 4 cups marshmallows

Instructions

1. **Melt Ingredients:**
    - In a large pot, melt butter and marshmallows over low heat, stirring until smooth.
2. **Add Cereal:**
    - Remove from heat and quickly stir in rice cereal until well coated.
3. **Press into Pan:**
    - Press the mixture into a greased 9x13 inch pan.
4. **Cool and Cut:**
    - Allow to cool before cutting into squares.

No-Bake Chocolate Oatmeal Cookies

Ingredients

- 1/2 cup peanut butter
- 1/2 cup honey or maple syrup
- 1/4 cup cocoa powder
- 2 cups oats
- 1 teaspoon vanilla extract

Instructions

1. **Combine Ingredients:**
   - In a bowl, mix peanut butter, honey, cocoa powder, oats, and vanilla until well combined.
2. **Form Cookies:**
   - Drop spoonfuls of the mixture onto a lined baking sheet.
3. **Chill:**
   - Refrigerate for at least 30 minutes to set.
4. **Store:**
   - Keep in an airtight container in the fridge for up to a week.

Strawberry Banana Nice Cream

Ingredients

- 2 ripe bananas, sliced and frozen
- 1 cup strawberries, frozen
- 1 tablespoon almond milk (or milk of choice)

Instructions

1. **Blend Ingredients:**
   - In a food processor, blend frozen bananas, strawberries, and almond milk until smooth and creamy.
2. **Serve:**
   - Scoop into bowls and enjoy immediately, or freeze for a firmer texture.

Enjoy your delicious treats!

Peanut Butter and Jelly Bites

Ingredients

- 1 cup oats
- 1/2 cup peanut butter
- 1/4 cup honey or maple syrup
- 1/4 cup your favorite fruit jam
- 1/2 teaspoon vanilla extract

Instructions

1. **Mix Ingredients:**
    - In a bowl, combine oats, peanut butter, honey, and vanilla extract. Mix until well combined.
2. **Form Bites:**
    - Scoop out portions and flatten them into discs. Add a small dollop of jam to the center of half of the discs and top with the other halves.
3. **Chill:**
    - Refrigerate for at least 30 minutes to firm up.
4. **Serve:**
    - Enjoy as a snack!

Chia Seed Pudding

Ingredients

- 1/4 cup chia seeds
- 1 cup almond milk (or milk of choice)
- 1 tablespoon maple syrup (optional)
- 1/2 teaspoon vanilla extract

Instructions

1. **Combine Ingredients:**
    - In a bowl, whisk together chia seeds, almond milk, maple syrup, and vanilla.
2. **Chill:**
    - Refrigerate for at least 4 hours or overnight, stirring occasionally.
3. **Serve:**
    - Enjoy topped with fruit or nuts!

No-Bake Oreo Truffles

Ingredients

- 1 package Oreo cookies (about 15 cookies)
- 8 oz cream cheese, softened
- 8 oz chocolate (for coating)

Instructions

1. **Crush Oreos:**
    - In a food processor, crush Oreo cookies until fine crumbs remain.
2. **Mix with Cream Cheese:**
    - Add cream cheese and mix until well combined.
3. **Form Balls:**
    - Roll the mixture into small balls and place on a baking sheet.
4. **Chill:**
    - Refrigerate for 30 minutes to set.
5. **Coat with Chocolate:**
    - Melt chocolate and dip each truffle, then return to the baking sheet to harden.

Energy-Boosting Granola Bars

Ingredients

- 2 cups rolled oats
- 1/2 cup nut butter (peanut or almond)
- 1/4 cup honey or maple syrup
- 1/4 cup nuts (chopped)
- 1/4 cup dried fruit (optional)

Instructions

1. **Preheat Oven:**
    - Preheat your oven to 350°F (175°C). Line a baking dish with parchment paper.
2. **Mix Ingredients:**
    - In a bowl, combine all ingredients until well mixed.
3. **Press into Pan:**
    - Spread the mixture evenly into the prepared baking dish and press down firmly.
4. **Bake:**
    - Bake for 15-20 minutes until golden brown.
5. **Cool and Cut:**
    - Allow to cool before cutting into bars.

Chocolate-Dipped Fruit

Ingredients

- 1 cup fresh fruit (strawberries, bananas, or apple slices)
- 1 cup chocolate chips (dark or milk)

Instructions

1. **Melt Chocolate:**
    - In a microwave-safe bowl, melt chocolate chips in 30-second intervals until smooth.
2. **Dip Fruit:**
    - Dip each piece of fruit into the melted chocolate, allowing excess to drip off.
3. **Set:**
    - Place on a baking sheet lined with parchment paper and refrigerate until chocolate hardens.
4. **Serve:**
    - Enjoy as a sweet snack!

Vanilla Yogurt Parfaits

Ingredients

- 2 cups vanilla yogurt
- 1 cup granola
- 1 cup mixed berries (strawberries, blueberries, raspberries)

Instructions

1. **Layer Ingredients:**
    - In serving cups, layer yogurt, granola, and mixed berries.
2. **Repeat Layers:**
    - Repeat until all ingredients are used.
3. **Serve:**
    - Enjoy immediately!

Nutty Trail Mix Clusters

Ingredients

- 1 cup mixed nuts
- 1/2 cup dried fruit
- 1/4 cup nut butter
- 1/4 cup honey or maple syrup

Instructions

1. **Combine Ingredients:**
   - In a bowl, mix nuts, dried fruit, nut butter, and honey until well combined.
2. **Form Clusters:**
   - Scoop out portions and form clusters on a baking sheet.
3. **Chill:**
   - Refrigerate for 30 minutes to set.
4. **Serve:**
   - Enjoy as a snack!

Chocolate Avocado Mousse

Ingredients

- 2 ripe avocados
- 1/4 cup cocoa powder
- 1/4 cup maple syrup
- 1 teaspoon vanilla extract

Instructions

1. **Blend Ingredients:**
   - In a food processor, blend avocados, cocoa powder, maple syrup, and vanilla until smooth.
2. **Chill:**
   - Transfer to a bowl and refrigerate for at least 30 minutes.
3. **Serve:**
   - Enjoy chilled, optionally topped with berries or nuts!

Enjoy your delicious treats!

No-Bake Peanut Butter Pie

Ingredients

- 1 1/2 cups graham cracker crumbs
- 1/2 cup melted coconut oil
- 1 cup peanut butter
- 1 cup powdered sugar
- 1 cup whipped cream (or coconut whipped cream)
- 1 teaspoon vanilla extract

Instructions

1. **Prepare Crust:**
   - In a bowl, mix graham cracker crumbs and melted coconut oil. Press into the bottom of a pie dish.
2. **Make Filling:**
   - In another bowl, beat peanut butter, powdered sugar, whipped cream, and vanilla until smooth. Spread over the crust.
3. **Chill:**
   - Refrigerate for at least 4 hours or until set.
4. **Serve:**
   - Slice and enjoy!

Coconut-Lime Energy Bites

Ingredients

- 1 cup rolled oats
- 1/2 cup shredded coconut
- 1/4 cup almond butter
- 1/4 cup honey or maple syrup
- Zest of 1 lime
- Juice of 1 lime

Instructions

1. **Mix Ingredients:**
    - In a bowl, combine all ingredients until well mixed.
2. **Form Bites:**
    - Scoop out portions and roll into balls.
3. **Chill:**
    - Refrigerate for at least 30 minutes to set.
4. **Serve:**
    - Enjoy as a snack!

S'mores Bites

Ingredients

- 1 cup graham cracker crumbs
- 1/2 cup mini marshmallows
- 1/2 cup chocolate chips
- 1/4 cup coconut oil, melted

Instructions

1. **Combine Ingredients:**
    - In a bowl, mix graham cracker crumbs, marshmallows, chocolate chips, and melted coconut oil.
2. **Form Bites:**
    - Press the mixture into a lined baking dish and refrigerate for 30 minutes.
3. **Cut and Serve:**
    - Cut into squares and enjoy!

Date and Nut Balls

Ingredients

- 1 cup pitted dates
- 1 cup nuts (almonds, walnuts, or pecans)
- 1/4 cup cocoa powder
- 1 teaspoon vanilla extract

Instructions

1. **Blend Ingredients:**
   - In a food processor, blend dates, nuts, cocoa powder, and vanilla until a sticky mixture forms.
2. **Form Balls:**
   - Scoop out portions and roll into balls.
3. **Chill:**
   - Refrigerate for at least 30 minutes to set.
4. **Serve:**
   - Enjoy as a healthy snack!

Pumpkin Spice Bites

Ingredients

- 1 cup rolled oats
- 1/2 cup pumpkin puree
- 1/4 cup almond butter
- 1/4 cup honey or maple syrup
- 1 teaspoon pumpkin spice
- 1/4 cup chocolate chips (optional)

Instructions

1. **Mix Ingredients:**
    - In a bowl, combine all ingredients until well mixed.
2. **Form Bites:**
    - Scoop out portions and roll into balls.
3. **Chill:**
    - Refrigerate for at least 30 minutes to set.
4. **Serve:**
    - Enjoy as a tasty treat!

No-Bake Lemon Bars

Ingredients

- 1 1/2 cups almond flour
- 1/4 cup coconut oil, melted
- 1/4 cup honey or maple syrup
- 1/2 cup lemon juice
- Zest of 1 lemon
- 1/4 cup coconut cream

Instructions

1. **Prepare Crust:**
   - In a bowl, mix almond flour, melted coconut oil, and honey. Press into the bottom of a lined baking dish.
2. **Make Filling:**
   - In another bowl, whisk together lemon juice, lemon zest, and coconut cream. Pour over the crust.
3. **Chill:**
   - Refrigerate for at least 4 hours or until set.
4. **Cut and Serve:**
   - Cut into bars and enjoy!

Chocolate Coconut Bliss Balls

Ingredients

- 1 cup shredded coconut
- 1/2 cup cocoa powder
- 1/4 cup almond butter
- 1/4 cup honey or maple syrup
- 1 teaspoon vanilla extract

Instructions

1. **Mix Ingredients:**
   - In a bowl, combine all ingredients until well mixed.
2. **Form Balls:**
   - Scoop out portions and roll into balls.
3. **Chill:**
   - Refrigerate for at least 30 minutes to set.
4. **Serve:**
   - Enjoy as a delicious treat!

Frozen Yogurt Bark

Ingredients

- 2 cups yogurt (Greek or regular)
- 1/2 cup mixed berries
- 1/4 cup granola
- 1 tablespoon honey (optional)

Instructions

1. **Prepare Yogurt Mixture:**
    - In a bowl, mix yogurt with honey if using.
2. **Spread on Baking Sheet:**
    - Spread yogurt evenly on a lined baking sheet.
3. **Top with Toppings:**
    - Sprinkle berries and granola on top.
4. **Freeze:**
    - Freeze for at least 2 hours or until firm.
5. **Break and Serve:**
    - Break into pieces and enjoy!

Enjoy these delicious no-bake treats!

Layered Pudding Cups

Ingredients

- 2 cups chocolate pudding (store-bought or homemade)
- 2 cups vanilla pudding (store-bought or homemade)
- 1 cup whipped cream
- Fresh berries (for topping)

Instructions

1. **Layer Puddings:**
    - In serving cups, alternate layers of chocolate pudding and vanilla pudding.
2. **Top with Whipped Cream:**
    - Add a layer of whipped cream on top.
3. **Garnish:**
    - Top with fresh berries before serving.

Matcha Green Tea Energy Bites

Ingredients

- 1 cup rolled oats
- 1/4 cup nut butter (almond or peanut)
- 1/4 cup honey or maple syrup
- 2 tablespoons matcha powder
- 1/4 cup shredded coconut (optional)

Instructions

1. **Mix Ingredients:**
    - In a bowl, combine all ingredients until well mixed.
2. **Form Bites:**
    - Scoop out portions and roll into balls.
3. **Chill:**
    - Refrigerate for at least 30 minutes to set.
4. **Serve:**
    - Enjoy as a healthy snack!

No-Bake Fruit Tart

Ingredients

- 1 1/2 cups graham cracker crumbs
- 1/2 cup melted coconut oil
- 1 cup cream cheese (or vegan alternative)
- 1/2 cup powdered sugar
- 2 cups mixed fresh fruit (berries, kiwi, etc.)

Instructions

1. **Prepare Crust:**
   - In a bowl, mix graham cracker crumbs and melted coconut oil. Press into the bottom of a tart pan.
2. **Make Filling:**
   - In another bowl, beat cream cheese and powdered sugar until smooth. Spread over the crust.
3. **Top with Fruit:**
   - Arrange mixed fruit on top of the filling.
4. **Chill:**
   - Refrigerate for at least 2 hours before serving.

Chocolate Hazelnut Spread Dip

Ingredients

- 1/2 cup chocolate hazelnut spread
- 1/2 cup cream cheese, softened
- 1 tablespoon milk (or more for desired consistency)
- Fresh fruit or graham crackers (for dipping)

Instructions

1. **Mix Ingredients:**
    - In a bowl, combine chocolate hazelnut spread, cream cheese, and milk. Mix until smooth.
2. **Serve:**
    - Transfer to a serving dish and enjoy with fresh fruit or graham crackers.

Peanut Butter Chocolate Chip Dip

Ingredients

- 1/2 cup peanut butter
- 1/2 cup cream cheese, softened
- 1/4 cup honey or maple syrup
- 1/4 cup chocolate chips

Instructions

1. **Mix Ingredients:**
    - In a bowl, combine peanut butter, cream cheese, and honey until smooth. Fold in chocolate chips.
2. **Serve:**
    - Serve with apple slices, pretzels, or crackers.

No-Bake Rice Pudding

Ingredients

- 1 cup cooked rice
- 1 cup milk (or almond milk)
- 1/4 cup sugar
- 1 teaspoon vanilla extract
- 1 teaspoon cinnamon
- Raisins (optional)

Instructions

1. **Combine Ingredients:**
    - In a bowl, mix cooked rice, milk, sugar, vanilla, and cinnamon. Stir until well combined.
2. **Add Raisins:**
    - Fold in raisins if using.
3. **Chill:**
    - Refrigerate for at least 1 hour before serving.
4. **Serve:**
    - Enjoy chilled!

Berry Coconut Smoothie Pops

Ingredients

- 2 cups mixed berries (fresh or frozen)
- 1 cup coconut yogurt (or regular yogurt)
- 1 tablespoon honey (optional)

Instructions

1. **Blend Ingredients:**
    - In a blender, combine berries, coconut yogurt, and honey. Blend until smooth.
2. **Pour into Molds:**
    - Pour the mixture into popsicle molds.
3. **Freeze:**
    - Freeze for at least 4 hours or until solid.
4. **Serve:**
    - Remove from molds and enjoy!

Chocolate-Covered Pretzel Bites

Ingredients

- 1 cup pretzel twists
- 1 cup chocolate chips (dark or milk)
- Sea salt (optional)

Instructions

1. **Melt Chocolate:**
   - In a microwave-safe bowl, melt chocolate chips in 30-second intervals until smooth.
2. **Dip Pretzels:**
   - Dip each pretzel into the melted chocolate and place on a baking sheet lined with parchment paper.
3. **Sprinkle with Salt:**
   - If desired, sprinkle sea salt on top.
4. **Chill:**
   - Refrigerate until chocolate hardens, then enjoy!

Enjoy these delightful treats!

Oatmeal Cookie Dough Bites

Ingredients

- 1 cup rolled oats
- 1/2 cup almond flour
- 1/2 cup peanut butter
- 1/4 cup maple syrup
- 1/2 teaspoon vanilla extract
- 1/4 cup chocolate chips

Instructions

1. **Mix Ingredients:**
    - In a bowl, combine all ingredients until well mixed.
2. **Form Bites:**
    - Scoop out portions and roll into balls.
3. **Chill:**
    - Refrigerate for at least 30 minutes to set.
4. **Serve:**
    - Enjoy as a snack!

Nut-Free Granola Bars

Ingredients

- 2 cups rolled oats
- 1/2 cup sunflower seed butter
- 1/4 cup honey or maple syrup
- 1/4 cup dried fruit (raisins, cranberries, etc.)
- 1/4 cup mini chocolate chips (optional)

Instructions

1. **Preheat Oven:**
   - Preheat your oven to 350°F (175°C). Line a baking dish with parchment paper.
2. **Mix Ingredients:**
   - In a bowl, combine all ingredients until well mixed.
3. **Press into Pan:**
   - Spread the mixture evenly into the prepared baking dish and press down firmly.
4. **Bake:**
   - Bake for 15-20 minutes until golden brown.
5. **Cool and Cut:**
   - Allow to cool before cutting into bars.

No-Bake Banana Cream Pie

Ingredients

- 1 1/2 cups graham cracker crumbs
- 1/4 cup coconut oil, melted
- 2 ripe bananas, sliced
- 1 cup vanilla pudding (store-bought or homemade)
- Whipped cream (for topping)

Instructions

1. **Prepare Crust:**
    - In a bowl, mix graham cracker crumbs and melted coconut oil. Press into the bottom of a pie dish.
2. **Layer Pudding and Bananas:**
    - Spread vanilla pudding over the crust and layer with banana slices.
3. **Top with Whipped Cream:**
    - Add whipped cream on top.
4. **Chill:**
    - Refrigerate for at least 2 hours before serving.

Mint Chocolate Chip Energy Bites

Ingredients

- 1 cup rolled oats
- 1/2 cup almond butter
- 1/4 cup honey or maple syrup
- 1/4 cup mini chocolate chips
- 1 teaspoon peppermint extract

Instructions

1. **Mix Ingredients:**
   - In a bowl, combine all ingredients until well mixed.
2. **Form Bites:**
   - Scoop out portions and roll into balls.
3. **Chill:**
   - Refrigerate for at least 30 minutes to set.
4. **Serve:**
   - Enjoy as a refreshing snack!

Chocolate Chip Cookie Pie

Ingredients

- 1 cup all-purpose flour
- 1/2 cup brown sugar
- 1/2 cup granulated sugar
- 1/2 cup butter, softened
- 1/2 cup chocolate chips
- 1 egg
- 1 teaspoon vanilla extract

Instructions

1. **Preheat Oven:**
    - Preheat your oven to 350°F (175°C). Grease a pie dish.
2. **Mix Ingredients:**
    - In a bowl, cream together butter, brown sugar, and granulated sugar. Beat in the egg and vanilla. Gradually add flour and mix until combined. Fold in chocolate chips.
3. **Bake:**
    - Spread the mixture into the prepared pie dish and bake for 25-30 minutes until golden brown.
4. **Cool and Serve:**
    - Allow to cool before slicing and serving.

No-Bake Chocolate Mousse Cups

Ingredients

- 1 cup dark chocolate chips
- 1 cup heavy cream
- 2 tablespoons sugar
- 1 teaspoon vanilla extract

Instructions

1. **Melt Chocolate:**
    - In a microwave-safe bowl, melt chocolate chips in 30-second intervals until smooth. Let cool slightly.
2. **Whip Cream:**
    - In a separate bowl, whip heavy cream, sugar, and vanilla until soft peaks form.
3. **Combine:**
    - Gently fold the melted chocolate into the whipped cream until well combined.
4. **Chill:**
    - Spoon into serving cups and refrigerate for at least 2 hours before serving.

Peanut Butter Banana Sushi

Ingredients

- 1 large banana
- 2 tablespoons peanut butter
- 1/4 cup granola or crushed nuts
- Honey (for drizzling, optional)

Instructions

1. **Spread Peanut Butter:**
    - Spread peanut butter evenly over the banana.
2. **Roll in Granola:**
    - Roll the peanut butter-covered banana in granola or crushed nuts.
3. **Slice:**
    - Slice into bite-sized pieces.
4. **Serve:**
    - Drizzle with honey if desired and enjoy!

Cinnamon Roll Energy Bites

Ingredients

- 1 cup rolled oats
- 1/2 cup almond butter
- 1/4 cup honey or maple syrup
- 1 teaspoon cinnamon
- 1/4 cup chopped nuts (optional)

Instructions

1. **Mix Ingredients:**
    - In a bowl, combine all ingredients until well mixed.
2. **Form Bites:**
    - Scoop out portions and roll into balls.
3. **Chill:**
    - Refrigerate for at least 30 minutes to set.
4. **Serve:**
    - Enjoy as a delicious snack!

Enjoy these tasty treats!

No-Bake Tiramisu Cups

Ingredients

- 1 cup strong brewed coffee, cooled
- 1 cup mascarpone cheese
- 1/2 cup heavy cream
- 1/4 cup sugar
- 1 teaspoon vanilla extract
- Ladyfinger cookies (or similar)
- Cocoa powder (for dusting)

Instructions

1. **Whip Cream:**
    - In a bowl, whip heavy cream, sugar, and vanilla until soft peaks form.
2. **Combine with Mascarpone:**
    - Gently fold mascarpone cheese into the whipped cream.
3. **Layer Cups:**
    - Dip ladyfingers briefly in coffee, then layer in serving cups. Top with mascarpone mixture.
4. **Repeat Layers:**
    - Repeat layers until cups are filled.
5. **Chill:**
    - Refrigerate for at least 4 hours. Dust with cocoa powder before serving.

Raspberry Coconut Bites

Ingredients

- 1 cup pitted dates
- 1 cup shredded coconut
- 1/2 cup raspberries (fresh or frozen)
- 1 tablespoon coconut oil

Instructions

1. **Blend Ingredients:**
   - In a food processor, combine dates, shredded coconut, raspberries, and coconut oil. Blend until a sticky mixture forms.
2. **Form Bites:**
   - Scoop out portions and roll into balls.
3. **Chill:**
   - Refrigerate for at least 30 minutes to set.
4. **Serve:**
   - Enjoy as a fruity snack!

Healthy Chocolate Fudge

Ingredients

- 1 cup nut butter (almond or peanut)
- 1/4 cup cocoa powder
- 1/4 cup honey or maple syrup
- 1 teaspoon vanilla extract

Instructions

1. **Mix Ingredients:**
     - In a bowl, combine nut butter, cocoa powder, honey, and vanilla. Mix until smooth.
2. **Transfer to Pan:**
     - Pour the mixture into a lined baking dish and spread evenly.
3. **Chill:**
     - Refrigerate for at least 2 hours until firm.
4. **Cut and Serve:**
     - Cut into squares and enjoy!

Caramel Apple Dip

Ingredients

- 1 cup cream cheese, softened
- 1/2 cup brown sugar
- 1/4 cup caramel sauce
- 1 teaspoon vanilla extract
- Sliced apples (for dipping)

Instructions

1. **Mix Ingredients:**
    - In a bowl, combine cream cheese, brown sugar, caramel sauce, and vanilla. Mix until smooth.
2. **Serve:**
    - Transfer to a serving dish and enjoy with sliced apples.

No-Bake Cherry Almond Bars

Ingredients

- 1 cup almonds (or almond flour)
- 1 cup pitted dates
- 1/2 cup dried cherries
- 1 tablespoon almond extract

Instructions

1. **Blend Ingredients:**
   - In a food processor, blend almonds, dates, dried cherries, and almond extract until a sticky mixture forms.
2. **Press into Pan:**
   - Press the mixture into a lined baking dish and flatten.
3. **Chill:**
   - Refrigerate for at least 1 hour.
4. **Cut and Serve:**
   - Cut into bars and enjoy!

Sliced Fruit with Nut Butter

Ingredients

- Assorted fresh fruit (apples, bananas, pears, etc.)
- Nut butter (peanut, almond, or cashew)

Instructions

1. **Slice Fruit:**
     - Slice your choice of fruit.
2. **Serve:**
     - Arrange on a plate and serve with nut butter for dipping.

No-Bake Chocolate Chip Cheesecake

Ingredients

- 1 1/2 cups graham cracker crumbs
- 1/2 cup melted butter
- 1 cup cream cheese, softened
- 1/2 cup powdered sugar
- 1 teaspoon vanilla extract
- 1/2 cup mini chocolate chips

Instructions

1. **Prepare Crust:**
   - In a bowl, mix graham cracker crumbs and melted butter. Press into the bottom of a pie dish.
2. **Mix Filling:**
   - In another bowl, beat cream cheese, powdered sugar, and vanilla until smooth. Fold in chocolate chips.
3. **Spread Filling:**
   - Pour the mixture into the crust and smooth the top.
4. **Chill:**
   - Refrigerate for at least 4 hours before serving.

Blueberry Coconut Chia Pudding

Ingredients

- 1/4 cup chia seeds
- 1 cup coconut milk
- 1 tablespoon honey or maple syrup
- 1/2 cup fresh blueberries

Instructions

1. **Combine Ingredients:**
    - In a bowl, mix chia seeds, coconut milk, and honey. Stir well.
2. **Chill:**
    - Refrigerate for at least 4 hours or overnight until thickened.
3. **Serve:**
    - Top with fresh blueberries before serving and enjoy!

Enjoy these delightful recipes!

Gingerbread Energy Bites

Ingredients

- 1 cup rolled oats
- 1/2 cup almond butter
- 1/4 cup maple syrup
- 1 teaspoon ground ginger
- 1 teaspoon cinnamon
- 1/4 teaspoon nutmeg
- 1/4 teaspoon salt
- 1/4 cup chopped nuts or chocolate chips (optional)

Instructions

1. **Mix Ingredients:**
    - In a bowl, combine all ingredients until well mixed.
2. **Form Bites:**
    - Scoop out portions and roll into balls.
3. **Chill:**
    - Refrigerate for at least 30 minutes to set.
4. **Serve:**
    - Enjoy as a healthy snack!

Vegan Coconut Lime Truffles

Ingredients

- 1 cup shredded coconut
- 1/2 cup coconut cream
- 1/4 cup maple syrup
- Zest of 1 lime
- Juice of 1 lime
- 1/2 cup melted dark chocolate (for coating)

Instructions

1. **Mix Ingredients:**
   - In a bowl, combine shredded coconut, coconut cream, maple syrup, lime zest, and lime juice until well mixed.
2. **Form Truffles:**
   - Scoop out portions and roll into balls.
3. **Chill:**
   - Refrigerate for at least 30 minutes to set.
4. **Coat in Chocolate:**
   - Dip each truffle in melted dark chocolate and place on a lined baking sheet.
5. **Chill Again:**
   - Refrigerate until the chocolate hardens, then enjoy!

Chocolate-Covered Banana Bites

Ingredients

- 2 ripe bananas
- 1 cup dark chocolate chips
- 1 tablespoon coconut oil
- Sea salt (for sprinkling, optional)

Instructions

1. **Slice Bananas:**
   - Slice bananas into bite-sized pieces.
2. **Melt Chocolate:**
   - In a microwave-safe bowl, melt chocolate chips and coconut oil in 30-second intervals until smooth.
3. **Dip Banana Slices:**
   - Dip each banana slice into the melted chocolate and place on a lined baking sheet.
4. **Sprinkle with Salt:**
   - If desired, sprinkle with sea salt.
5. **Chill:**
   - Refrigerate until the chocolate hardens, then enjoy!

Enjoy these delicious treats!

www.ingramcontent.com/pod-product-compliance
Lightning Source LLC
LaVergne TN
LVHW081336060526
838201LV00055B/2677